FELIX MENDELSSOHN BARTHOLDY

BODLEIAN LIBRARY · OXFORD

Bodleian Picture Books
Special Series No. 3

© BODLEIAN LIBRARY 1972

FIRST PUBLISHED 1972

SBN 900177 15 2

PRINTED IN GREAT BRITAIN
AT THE UNIVERSITY PRESS, OXFORD
BY VIVIAN RIDLER
PRINTER TO THE UNIVERSITY

PREFACE

W H E N Mendelssohn's reputation was established, his father, Abraham Mendelssohn, remarked that he used to be the son of his father, now he was the father of his son ('Früher war ich der Sohn meines Vaters, jetzt bin ich der Vater meines Sohnes'). He was proud of both, but pride in the influential part that the philosopher Moses Mendelssohn had taken in the recent history of Judaism did not prevent his choosing a Christian upbringing for his own children. They were given the name Mendelssohn Bartholdy, after their mother's Christian brother, Jacob Salomon Bartholdy. Abraham and his wife Lea waited until 1823 to be baptized themselves, and to take the double name.

They lived first at Hamburg, where their eldest children were born: Fanny in 1805; Jacob Ludwig Felix, 3 February 1809; and Rebecka, 1811. When Felix was three the family moved to Berlin, where Paul was born in 1813. Here their house became the meeting-place for innumerable visitors, many of them distinguished as scholars, writers, or thinkers, and in particular for people who shared their interest in music, books, the theatre, and the visual arts. There grew up a custom of Sunday music, in which the children took part, and the other performers included artists visiting the Prussian capital, as well as some of the city's own professional and amateur musicians. In 1825 Abraham bought a big house in Leipziger Strasse, with a leafy garden and a great 'garden room' at the back, to contain the lively and sociable activities of his family.

Among the visitors in 1821, when Felix was twelve, was the painter Carl Begas, introduced to the family by the uncle Bartholdy (for this uncle, see note on plate 15). Lea wrote to her cousin Henrietta von Pereira-Arnstein in enthusiasm about this 'quite heavenly man and painter' ('ganz himmlischer Mensch und Maler'), whose love of music had drawn him into the company and friendship of her children. His portrait sketch of Felix is plate 1.

Another visitor in the same year was the outrageous, but evidently lovable, French violinist, Alexandre Boucher, with his wife Céleste, on their way to Poland and Russia. Boucher gave Felix an album in which was pasted T. Cook's engraving of Mozart from Carmontelle's family portrait, 'Compositeur et Maitre de Musique, agé de 7 ans'. He inscribed the album 'Souvenir à son ami Félix (ou plutot Phénix, agé de 12 ans) digne rejeton des Mendelssohn'. Felix kept it till the end of his life, collecting in it pictures and musical 'album leaves', bringing it out to receive the contributions of friends and colleagues, and in particular of musicians whom he met on his travels, or with whom he had enjoyed working. Among its contents are the pieces shown on plates 3*b*, 3*c*, and 4. It was a memorial of friendship, and of the musical or artistic gifts of friends, of a kind which the family treasured. The elder sister, Fanny, was delighted with the present of a similar *album amicorum* a month or two later, and wrote thanking the cousin who gave it, 'Felix, my best friend, shall make a beginning, and has already composed a lovely piece which he is going to copy into it'. For a Christmas present to his fiancée in 1836 Felix prepared a rather more elaborate album, pasting into it precious things from his own collection (plates 5, 16, 20, 21) and gathering contributions from the family of his future wife. Still another album, even larger and grander, was her present for Christmas 1844, when the first was nearly full (plate 30).

The Mendelssohns were devoted and conscientious parents. Lea began to teach Felix the piano when he was six, and two years later, when he had passed through all the classes of the Elementarschule, and a tutor was giving him lessons at home, he was sent with Fanny for composition to Professor Zelter, the Principal of the new Berlin Singakademie, in his younger years known to Moses Mendelssohn. Zelter was close to the direct line of musical descent from J. S. Bach, his master having been Karl Friedrich Christian Fasch, who was the very junior colleague of Bach's son Carl Philipp Emanuel in the service of Frederick the Great; there was also a connection with Johann Philipp Kirnberger, who (for however brief a time) was actually a pupil of Sebastian Bach. To Zelter's introduc-tion of Bach's music to Felix may be traced the English Bach revival later in the nineteenth century (cf. note to plate 10).

Zelter must have loved Felix. In Lea's letters to her cousin there are glimpses of him taking part in family performances of the very early compositions, not at all on his dignity, and playing with the children. At supper on Felix's fifteenth birthday, Zelter proclaimed that they were no longer master and pupil, but colleagues: 'My dear son, . . . I make you my fellow in the name of Mozart, in the name of Haydn, and in the name of the old Bach' (the not irreverent parody is rhythmically clearer in the German). Within three years of this consecration, the Octet for strings and the Overture to *A Midsummer Night's Dream* (plate 7) had justified Zelter's confident satisfaction.

Earlier, in November 1821, Zelter had taken Felix to visit Goethe (plate 5), who was then in his seventy-third year. It was an occasion of intense pleasure to everyone concerned. Zelter wrote on 26 October: 'I would like to bring . . . my best pupil into your presence before I depart from this world (in which indeed I mean to continue as long as possible).' Goethe tested his friend's pupil by setting before him leaves from his collection of autograph music. Mozart's hand was read and played without difficulty. Beethoven, who according to Zelter 'always writes as if he used a besom and then wiped his sleeve over the wet ink' (plate 20), presented a harder problem, and Goethe was enchanted with Felix's success after only one preliminary trial. Felix improvised on the piano, and played— 'much more than at home', he wrote to his parents, 'seldom less than four hours, sometimes six, and in fact even as much as eight'. A memento from one of the ladies of Weimar, which Felix stuck into Boucher's album, is reproduced as plate 4. Goethe wrote to Abraham Mendelssohn of the quietness and dullness that had come over his house when this visit ended, accentuating for him the gloom of the short and stormy winter days. There were three other visits before Goethe died in 1832.

In 1822 Lea, who loathed travelling, gave in to Abraham (she once called him 'das *perpetuum mobile*') and undertook a family holiday in Switzerland. On this journey Felix was at last able to devote time to drawing, for which he had shown an inclination since early days. It appears that there was difficulty in keeping him occupied: 'My Felix has discovered a new source of pleasure in drawing the beautiful places where we were staying. As he is so lively that he must always be busy—and this was not always easily arranged on our voyage up the Rhine—his father offered him sketching as an amusement, and in a short time he has become quite skilful.' They gave him a large and a small drawing-book of the best English paper, each with his name 'FELIX' in gold on the cover. Always after this a sketch-book was an indispensable part of his holiday luggage (plates 8, 9, 11–15, 17–19). One of his first drawings is reproduced as plate 6. Towards the end of the holiday he sketched Mont Blanc 'at 4 in the morning'. On his more famous travels of 1829–32 this family journey was often in his mind, and in a letter home on 14 August 1831 he recalls his early feelings, and goes on to describe a change in his out- look: 'The mountains had dwelt in my memory only as vast jagged peaks, for their great altitude had entirely overwhelmed me. Today it was their immense extent, their solid spacious masses, the interconnection of all these huge piles—how they are related one to another, how they stand holding hands, this moved me specially today. Then think of all the glaciers, all the snowfields, all the rocky peaks dazzlingly lit and shining, and the far summits of distant ranges which reach over and peep through— I believe this is what God's thoughts look like.' In the three years of travel —in Scotland, Bavaria, Switzerland, and Italy—some of the excitability and swift susceptibility of his childhood had given way to a quieter, but no less responsive, power of contemplation.

The realization that Felix could have no other calling than music came early to his parents. A letter of Abraham's to Fanny—who, at fourteen, was learning to accept the fact that Felix, aged ten, had outstripped her—reflects their view: 'Music may perhaps be his calling, but for you it can only be an extra.' (All the same, she was able to discuss her brother's compositions with him in detail, and among the songs she later composed were some which he was content to print among his own: cf. note to plate 25.) 'Never can it, nor should it, be the ground-bass of your life and activity.' That was what it was to be for Felix, as his mother, with some misgiving, saw clearly on his next birthday at the performance of his first opera at Leipziger Strasse: 'It was a sight to warm a parent's heart, the beautiful child with his *Raphaelslocken* sitting among all those artists. . . . So his calling seems to be practically settled. . . . Heaven grant that it may be for his happiness. The way of an artist is nowadays indeed a thorny one.'

Lea's premonition was just. The first musical occasion outside the family circle was an unsuccessful performance, after exasperating delays, of a comic opera in 1827. Later experience in Berlin, with the single and magnificent exception of the St. Matthew Passion (plate 10), was never much happier. Against his own judgement, Felix became a candidate for Zelter's empty place at the Singakademie in 1832, and was not elected. But almost everywhere else he was successful and happy. He went first to Düsseldorf, where he spent two years as general music director, living in the house of the painter Wilhelm von Schadow (mentioned again in the notes to plates 3c, 15, 18, 19). In the autumn of 1835 he went to Leipzig in Saxony, and became Director of the Gewandhaus concerts (plate 24). This was a position of some prestige, and Mendelssohn was to add much to the distinction of Leipzig music, not only by his work at the Gewand-haus, but also by founding the Conservatorium, and by bringing the town to a fuller realization of its dignity as the home of J. S. Bach during the best years of his life as a composer. Fortunately Schumann (plate 24, note, and 31) was there to witness Mendelssohn's extraordinary and many-sided achievement, and articles in his *Neue Zeitschrift für Musik* reflect the elation of the musical part of the town during those energetic and happy years. Beyond what Schumann had to say of great, and often unknown, music, splendidly performed, the impact of the first performances of his own works under Mendelssohn's percipient direction must be remembered. After the first season at Leipzig (during which all of Beethoven's nine symphonies were performed) the University honoured Mendelssohn with the degree of Doctor of Philosophy, and other public honours from further afield followed (plate 23).

In 1841 there came an interruption from Berlin. The new King of Prussia, Frederick William IV, wanted Mendelssohn to take charge of the music in a projected Academy of Arts. In that same year he was appointed Kapellmeister both to King Frederick Augustus of Saxony and to the King of Prussia. The only course that seemed acceptable was to divide his time between the two places, and this he did for the next four years.

There were people who could continue some of his work at Leipzig in his absence—most notably the violinist Ferdinand David. David had known the Mendelssohns well in Berlin in 1827-9, and had led the second orchestra in the St. Matthew Passion there. After seven years in Russia, he saw Felix in Berlin at Abraham Mendelssohn's funeral in November 1835. Their friendship came to life again, and he was appointed leader of the Gewandhaus orchestra—a position which he filled most excellently, and in which he was to continue for thirty-seven years. It was for him, and indeed to some extent *with* him, that the violin concerto was composed. He was invaluable as a player of chamber music, which during Mendelssohn's directorship came to take a larger share in concerts at Leipzig. While Mendelssohn was away, he, with other musicians including Ferdinand Hiller and the young Dane, N. W. Gade, was able to maintain the character which his friend's hard work, sound judgement, and fastidious musicianship had given to the Gewandhaus concerts.

The work for which Mendelssohn was called away to Berlin proved frustrating and wearing, mainly because of the indecision of the authorities: there was uncertainty over the precise nature of his duties, and at times there was maddening delay before the performance of work which he had been harassed to prepare at speed. At last in 1844 he admitted that the strain was too great, resigned his post, and returned to the Gewandhaus and to his teaching at the Conservatorium. It was during the first winter after this that Jenny Lind first sang at Leipzig (plate 32).

Official duties left the summers comparatively free, and Mendelssohn was a good deal occupied with musical festivals throughout Germany (plate 28). These brought contacts with musicians who had not yet been to Leipzig, and no doubt also with many humbler professional and amateur musicians. In 1836, he spent some weeks of the summer at Frankfurt, conducting the amateur Cäcilien-Verein. Here, perhaps through his cousin Philipp Veit (cf. notes to plates 15 and 21), he met Cécile Jeanrenaud. They were married in March 1837. Cécile was not extraordinarily gifted, except as a devoted daughter, wife, and mother.

Her own mother was the widow of a Huguenot pastor. As the demands of Mendelssohn's profession grew in weight and complexity, time that could be spent peacefully with Cécile and their children became increasingly precious (plates 28, 29, notes).

Between 1829 and 1847 Mendelssohn was ten times in England, once accompanied by Cécile. On the first visit he conducted his own first symphony at the Philharmonic Society, where the work and its composer were received with great warmth. There were other musical engagements, and he enjoyed London and its sociable activities for four months, before setting out with his friend Karl Klingemann (who was in the Hanoverian diplomatic service in London) on their Scotch tour (plates 11, 12). The Hebrides overture and the Third Symphony, besides lesser works, were the outcome of his experiences on that occasion. In 1842 he was again the guest of the Philharmonic Society, and conducted the Scotch Symphony for them (plate 25). The first performance of any work of J. S. Bach in a Philharmonic concert was the D major suite, conducted by him in 1844. He was at the Birmingham Festival three times, for performances of his 'St. Paul', 1837, 'Hymn of Praise', 1840, and 'Elijah' (plate 33), 1846. He gave great pleasure to amateur musicians, the Queen herself among them (plate 25, note), and friendships were formed with several families besides those whose profession was music (plate 3*b*, note). He liked England and Scotland, and was very much liked in return. Perhaps his greatest service to British music was in the transmission, mainly through Sterndale Bennett, of his attitude to the music of J. S. Bach. Mendelssohn first saw Bennett as a boy of sixteen, playing his own violin concerto at the Academy of Music prize concert in 1833. As a young man Bennett several times stayed at Leipzig, one occasion being within the year of Mendelssohn's performance of the St. Matthew Passion (on 4 April 1841) in the Thomaskirche. Bennett founded the London Bach Society in 1849, and when, seven years after Mendelssohn's death, he gave the first English performance of the Passion in London, the work had been prepared from choral and orchestral parts used in Mendelssohn's own performance.

By 1847, Mendelssohn had packed into his thirty-eight years a long lifetime's activity: composition, and copying of music; playing and conducting; teaching; travelling; drawing; letter-writing (probably as many as 7,000 letters)—everything done with the most exacting care. And account can hardly be made of the pressures of family, friends, enemies (there were some), and colleagues. His sister Fanny died in May 1847, and the blow seemed to have been too heavy. Cécile took him to Switzerland with the children and other members of the family. There exists a sad little sketch-book in which he tried to return to his old holiday occupation, and completed nothing. But he did to some extent recover, enough to make a remarkable series of water-colour sketches, and to write his last string quartet (F minor, op. 80). The family went home to Leipzig in September, and there on 7 October he completed the song illustrated on plate 34. Soon after, he was taken ill, and after Cécile had nursed him through a series of increasingly violent attacks, he died late in the evening of 4 November. The subscription concert that evening had been cancelled, and on the next Thursday the concert was in memory of him, the first part consisting of his own music, the second the Eroica Symphony. Meanwhile, on the Sunday night, after receiving elaborate honours in Leipzig, Mendelssohn's coffin had been taken by train—with strange pauses for choral music, at midnight at Cöthen, at two in the morning at Dessau—to be buried in the family grave at Berlin.

Mendelssohn papers are in Oxford, not because of his own connections with England but because of those of his grandchildren. Descendants of both of his daughters were the friends of Miss Margaret Deneke of Gunfield, Oxford. Part of the collection which they entrusted to her now belongs to the Bodleian, and part is owned by her sister, Miss I I. C., Deneke.

The subjects for the plates are the choice of Peter Ward Jones, James Brister (who helped very much on artistic questions), and myself. It was Mr. Ward Jones who discovered the Chopin pieces where they had remained for so long unnoticed, and he has written some of the notes.

Thanks are due to Dr. Rudolf Elvers of the Mendelssohn Archiv, Berlin, for the answers to innumerable questions, and for his transcript of Lea Mendelssohn's letters to her cousin; to Lotte Labowsky and to Albi Rosenthal, for much help in reading, identifying, and translating; and to Charles Braybrooke for his photographic skill.

MARGARET CRUM

SELECT BIBLIOGRAPHY

Transcript of unpublished letters from Lea Mendelssohn to Henrietta von Pereira-Arnstein, made by Dr. Rudolf Elvers.

J. L. F. MENDELSSOHN-BARTHOLDY, *Briefe einer Reise*, [ed.] P. Sutermeister. Zürich, 1958.

—— *Briefwechsel mit . . . Karl Klingemann*, herausg. von K. Klingemann [the younger]. Essen, 1909.

SEBASTIAN HENSEL, *Die Familie Mendelssohn*. 3e Aufl. Berlin, 1882.

ERIC WERNER, *Mendelssohn*, tr. by D. Newlin. London, 1967.

PHILIP RADCLIFFE, *Mendelssohn*. Revised ed. (Master Musicians series.) London and New York, 1967.

ALFRED DÖRFFEL, *Geschichte der Gewandhausconcerte zu Leipzig, 1781–1881*. Leipzig, 1884.

MARTIN GECK, *Die Wiederentdeckung der Matthäus Passion im 19. Jahrhundert*. Regensburg, 1967.

Grove's History of Music and Musicians. London, 1879; and 5th ed., ed. by Eric Blom. London and New York, 1954.

Die Musik in Geschichte und Gegenwart, herausg. F. Blume. Kassel, etc., 1949–.

DESCRIPTION OF PLATES

1. MS. M. Deneke Mendelssohn e. 5. Oil sketch of F. M. B. in his thirteenth year, 1821, by Carl Begas.

This sketch and a preliminary cartoon were studies for a portrait, which was described by Lea as an excellent likeness and beautifully painted ('hinterliess er uns das schönste Andenken seines Meisterpinsels in einem höchst getroffenen und herrlich gemalten Bilde von Felix'). The portrait has now disappeared, but a photograph of it, and two pastel copies, survive. F. M. B.'s friend Dr. Johann Ludwig Casper, the librettist of his early operas, persuaded Begas to part with the oil sketch, which he did, though unwillingly, as he had hoped to use it in a historical painting. In 1896 Casper's daughters, who had no heirs, sent it to F. M. B.'s granddaughter Lili Wach, with three of his letters and a light-hearted sketch (3a).

2. F. M. B. Harmony exercise with C. F. Zelter, between 10 November and 13 December 1819. Owned by Miss H. C. Deneke.

Mendelssohn began his formal training in harmony and composition with Carl Friedrich Zelter in 1818. Zelter, who had been a friend of the family for many years, was an ideal teacher for the young Felix, with his interest in both musical education and the revival of music of the past, especially the works of Bach and Handel. Felix's early tuition followed a traditional course, which included the four-part harmonization of chorale melodies. Zelter provided the melody and added the note at the foot of the page—'Muss wenn der Bass fertig ist auf dem fortep. probirt und verbessert werden ohne dass die Correctur bemerkt wird'—'When the bass is finished, it must be tried out on the piano and improved, but without marking in the corrections.' Mendelssohn's own attempt at the exercise can be seen in the light pencilled notes, while the final version in ink was produced under Zelter's supervision.

3a. MS. M. Deneke Mendelssohn c. 32, fol. 8. Caricature by F. M. B. of himself and his younger brother Paul.

This sketch was kept by J. L. Casper together with the Begas oil sketch (1) and letters written by Felix while the Mendelssohn family was on holiday in Switzerland in the late summer of 1822 (cf. 6).

3b. MS. M. Deneke Mendelssohn d. 8, fol. 25. Anonymous sketch, probably of F. M. B., Wales, autumn 1829.

In the late summer of 1829, after his journey to Scotland with Karl Klingemann (cf. 11–12), F. M. B. visited the Taylor family at their country house Coed Du, between Mold and Ruthin, Flintshire. This picture was tucked into his album behind a drawing of Coed Du. The three 'Fantasien oder Capricen' for piano, op. 16, were composed for the daughters of the house: no. 1 was inspired by Anne's pinks (of which he hoped to take home seed), no. 3 by a stream enjoyed on a ride in Susan's company, and no. 2 by Honora's garland of the little orange trumpet flower *ecremocarpus*. The Taylors remembered the visit with delight, and Anne's account of it was printed in the first edition of Grove's *Dictionary of Music and Musicians*. F. M. B.'s memento is perhaps most likely to have been the work of Susan, who is described as being able to draw not only landscapes, but (as F. M. B. himself could not) men and women in the foregrounds.

3c. MS. M. Deneke Mendelssohn d. 8, fol. 30. Carl Sohn drawn by Eduard Bendemann, *c.* 1830–2.

F. M. B.'s journey to Italy in 1830 was in the company of three pupils of Wilhelm von Schadow, then director of the Düsseldorf Academy of Art, Eduard Bendemann, Theodor Hildebrant, and Carl Sohn. Sohn seems to make no other appearance in F. M. B.'s life and letters—he neither wrote to him nor contributed to his album—but two pictures of him survived this journey, Bendemann's drawing and a mild caricature inside the cover of one of F. M. B.'s sketch-books.

4. MS. M. Deneke Mendelssohn d. 8, fol. 31. Silhouette, 'Jacob's Ladder', by Adèle Schopenhauer (younger sister of the philosopher Arthur S.) given to F. M. B. (whose full name was Jacob Ludwig Felix) during his first visit to Goethe at Weimar, 1821.

Adèle Schopenhauer's explanation of the silhouette was as follows: 'Jacob, in his dream, saw a ladder reaching up to heaven, with angels ascending and descending on it; the ladder is still standing upon earth, and the ascending and descending angels are the notes which carry the sounds up to heaven.' (The German for the musical scale is *Tonleiter*, literally, *note-ladder*.)

5. MS. M. Deneke Mendelssohn c. 21, fol. 6. Pen-and-ink sketch by Goethe of the death of Eurydice, with a signature cut from a letter.

It was appropriate for Felix to have a drawing connected with Orpheus, but it is not clear whether or not Goethe himself gave it to him. In an essay written by Goethe many years before his meeting with Felix (published in *Propyläen*, vol. i, 1798, 'Über Laocoon'), he was considering pathos in sculpture, and chose as illustration the subject of this drawing: 'Think of Eurydice, in the moment when, walking cheerfully across the meadow carrying the flowers she has gathered, she steps on a snake and is bitten in the heel. She would make an affecting statue, if one could express the tension between her cheerful progress and her painful arrest, by the way she drops the flowers, by the attitude of her limbs as well as by the movement of the drapery.'

6. MS. M. Deneke Mendelssohn c. 5, fol. 4. 'Wattwyl im Canton St. Gallen, 3 August 1822.'

This is one of the earlier among forty-two sketches done by Felix (then aged 13) on the family holiday in Switzerland, July–October 1822. At Wattwyl they had thunder and lightning, but friendly folk at the inn, as he wrote to Dr. J. L. Casper (cf. 1).

7. Overture to *A Midsummer Night's Dream* (op. 21). Owned by Miss H. C. Deneke. An early, perhaps even first, draft in full score, headed at the top right-hand corner, according to F. M. B.'s practice, 'H[ilf] d[u] m[ir]'. 8 leaves, containing 127 bars only. Probably written July 1826. The final completed score was dated 6 August 1826. F. M. B.'s friend and fellow pupil under Zelter, A. B. Marx, claimed that drastic revision of the original score was undertaken on his advice: 'The introductory chords and the dance of the elves were just as we know them. Then, alas, there followed the overture proper. . . . I was unable to associate it with *A Midsummer Night's Dream*.' After a brief offended pause, F. M. B. wrote to Marx: 'You are right in every respect. But now come and help.' Marx says: 'Only the allusion to the lovers' wanderings in the first motif (E, D♯, D, C♯) could be salvaged from the original; everything else had to be rewritten. . . . "It's too mad, too absurd" he shouted, when I insisted on his saving a place for the jesters and even for Bottom's ardent braying.' There is not enough of the present draft to throw much light on Marx's story: the fairies' dance differs only in very small points from the score as it was printed; for what Tovey calls 'the world of festive daylight' bursting in at bar 61, there stood 34 bars which were totally rejected; and the last three pages here surviving were clearly working towards bars 96–132 of the final version. Whatever stage in the composition is represented, this early score shows that F. M. B. knew very early the manner in which the mysterious scene was to be set and the elves should dance. He saw no reason to change when the music was brought to light again in 1843, when the old overture and some new pieces commissioned by the King of Prussia were performed as accompaniment to a production of the play at Potsdam.

8, 9. MS. M. Deneke Mendelssohn d. 9, fols. 5 and 15. 'Coburg 3 Sept. 1827' and 'Coblenz 5 Oct. 1827'.

Two pencil drawings from the sketch-book which F. M. B. took on a holiday (as he wrote to Klingemann, 'allein!'—that is, without his family) with two student friends. Parts only of his letters to his family have yet been published. They reflect a return to cheerfulness, after the death of a friend and the dispiriting effect of the single performance earlier in the year of his opera *The Wedding of Camacho*. 'We get on together quite as well as we enjoy ourselves, and that is saying a great deal. Our talk is alternately of musicians, fevers, and Homer, so each has his own topic, and in a student song and refrain we all join in one.' At Heidelberg F. M. B. made the acquaintance of A. F. J. Thibaut, author of *Ueber Reinheit der Tonkunst*, 1825 (translated as *Purity in Musical Art* by W. H. Gladstone, son of W. E. G.), founder of a Palestrina Society, and owner of a fine collection of music. F. M. B. told him 'he did not yet know the fountainhead and the most important things in music, because all that was comprised in Sebastian [Bach]. He said, when I left him, "Farewell, and we will build our friendship on Luis de Vittoria and Sebastian Bach, like the two lovers who promise each other to look at the moon, and then fancy they are near each other."' The holiday ended with a journey by boat from Mainz to Cologne, and a visit to F. M. B.'s uncle Joseph Mendelssohn at Horchheim, near Coblenz, where they celebrated the vintage before leaving for a Handel oratorio performed by the Cäcilien-Verein at Frankfurt, and the journey home to Berlin.

10. Mendelssohn's score of the St. Matthew Passion of J. S. Bach. Owned by Miss H. C. Deneke.

The opening of the final chorus of the first part ('O Mensch, bewein' dein' Sünde gross') with F. M. B.'s pencilled marks. These refer to dynamics and to the realization of the through bass and to the substitution of clarinets for the oboi d'amore, the proper instruments not being available.

It seems that this score is derived from an early authoritative score—neither the autograph which Pölchau had from C. P. E. Bach, although he had it with him in Berlin from 1813, nor the earlier copy by Bach's son-in-law J. C. Altnikol, from which Zelter's score was derived. This score was given to Felix when he was fourteen by his grandmother Babette Salomon, for Christmas 1823. The copyist was Eduard Rietz, who played, and indeed for a while taught Felix, the violin, and was to lead the first orchestra when Felix conducted the work on 11 March 1829 at the Berlin Singakademie.

Zelter, whose support, as Directer of the Singakademie, was essential, was with difficulty persuaded to allow Felix to attempt a performance. He regarded the under-taking as too difficult. But his account of the performance in a letter to Goethe shows him completely won over. He sat near the orchestra, and followed his score. 'If only the old Bach could have heard our performance' ('Hätte doch der alte Bach unsre Ausführung hören konnen'). It was the first since Bach's death. Its traditions were carried on in England by Sterndale Bennett, to whom chorus and orchestral parts were lent to assist in rehearsing for the first English performance of the work, which took place in the Hanover Square Rooms, London, on 6 April 1854.

11, 12. MS. M. Deneke Mendelssohn d. 2, fols. 10 and 28. Two drawings from F. M. B.'s journey to Scotland with Karl Klingemann, 1829: Durham Cathedral from the west, and 'Ein Blick auf die Hebriden und Morven'.

The view towards the Hebrides was the inspiration of the Overture later called 'Die Fingalshöhle', op. 26. Klingemann provided verses for each picture. They made two copies of this record of their journey—a fact which probably accounts for the un-finished appearance of some of the drawings, including 12. Klingemann's copy is now in Sweden. F. M. B.'s copy was handed down to his granddaughter, Miss M. D. M. Benecke, and was generously given (with other sketch-books) to the Library by her friend Miss M. E. Andrews, to whom she had bequeathed it.

13. MS. M. Deneke Mendelssohn d. 2, fol. 40. Thomas Telford's suspension bridge at Conway, built 1822–6.

Drawn by F. M. B. on 26 August 1829, on his way back through Wales to London after parting from Klingemann at Liverpool. His diary contains a sketch of Telford's even greater achievement, the suspension bridge over the Menai Straits. Parting from Klingemann left him in low spirits ('bad service, exorbitant bills, my drawing a failure [he does not specify further] and such like vexations added to my discomfort'). To pass the time he investigated another piece of English engineering, the great railway tunnel under Liverpool, excavation of which under the direction of George Stephenson was completed only the summer before. 'I spoke to the inspector, and . . . prevailed upon him to allow me to go in a truck . . . to the harbour. The speed was fifteen miles an hour: . . . no horse, no engine, the carriage goes of its own accord, getting gradually quicker and quicker . . . the draught extinguished the lights. . . . For the first time in my life I saw *Nothing*. The truck tears on faster and faster, and rattles worse and worse—a trial to my nerves! . . . it was bitter cold. At last the warm red daylight streamed in at the further end, and when I alighted I stood by the harbour. I felt much relieved, and when on my way home I went through the market house the sight of it quite cheered me up.'

14. MS. M. Deneke Mendelssohn d. 10, fol. 5. 'Garmisch' and the 'Zugspitz', 27 July 1830.

F. M. B.'s journey to Italy began with a visit (the last) to Goethe at Weimar, and two months at Munich (6 June–7 August), interrupted by a brief holiday with A. B. Marx (cf. 7 n.) in the Bavarian Alps, apparently including Oberammergau and the Passion play. Marx had this holiday in mind in a chapter of his memoirs headed 'Die weite Welt', but their friendship was unhappily broken by then and he does not speak of F. M. B. in this connection. Plate 14 illustrates one of three sketches all begun on the same day of their holiday. In a letter written to his mother on 11 August F. M. B. reported one misfortune among others: 'I took up my pencil, and so entirely destroyed two of my favourite sketches taken in the Bavarian mountains, that I was obliged to tear them from my book, and to throw them out of the window.' The sketch-book appears to have been rebound on his return from Munich and shows no trace of the mutilation described to Lea.

15. MS. M. Deneke Mendelssohn d. 10, fol. 37. 'Bartholdys Haus an der Spanischen Treppe, [Rome], 24 Feb. 1831.'

Bartholdy, formerly Jacob Salomon, was Lea Mendelssohn's brother. He had taken the name on becoming a Christian. As Prussian Consul General in Rome he lived in the house on the right of this picture, the Palazzo Zuccari, which contains frescoes by its original owner, Federico Zuccaro. Bartholdy left his own mark of ownership: he came to the rescue of a little group of German artists (whose views were not very unlike those of the much later English Pre-Raphaelites)—his nephew, Philipp Veit, Peter Cornelius, J. F. Overbeck, and Wilhelm von Schadow—by inviting them to execute frescoes on the walls of one of the rooms. The theme they chose was the history of Joseph. Their work was later removed to the Nationalgalerie, Berlin. Bartholdy's sister-in-law, Henriette Mendelssohn, wrote to Lea: 'He ought to be Pope! Bartholdy I, like Leo X who also loved everything great and beautiful without counting the cost.' It was Bartholdy who introduced Begas to the family (cf. 1). He died in 1825.

16. MS. M. Deneke Mendelssohn c. 21, fol. 150. 'Bei Don Tommaso, Ischia, 21 May 1831', 'aus Eduard Bendemanns Skizzenbuch' (cf. 3*c*).

This sketch is in the album which F. M. B. gave to Cécile the Christmas between their engagement and wedding, 1836. A letter to his family dated 6 June 1831 describes the occasion when for a whole day rain forced him and his friends to shelter under an archway and sketch: 'I was not embarrassed, but sketched away with them, and I believe profited in some degree from it' (the other three were all studying art). His own picture, of the same view framed in the archway, was made from a little further to the right. He admits that the day would have been boring if they had not been in the prettiest poultry yard to be found in Europe, and another of his pictures shows it all—the orange tree, the white stone steps with pots of flowers, and the archway—from the other side, with tools for farm and garden and a suggestion of Don Tommaso's cocks and hens.

17. MS. M. Deneke Mendelssohn d. 3, fol. 16. Amalfi, 31 May 1831.
At this point in the sketch-book several drawings extend over the whole opening, and the headland and sea horizon have here been, unfortunately but unavoidably, cut off.

18, 19. MS. M. Deneke Mendelssohn d. 11, fols. 5 and 7. 'Der klyne Groenmarkt, Haag. 21 Aug. 1836', water-colour touched with gold, and 'Dampfboot der Zeeuw. 24 Aug. 1836', pencil drawing.

F. M. B. went to the Hague and Scheveningen for most of August with his friend Wilhelm von Schadow (cf. 3*c*) and Schadow's young son. This was a deliberate plan to be away from Frankfurt, where he had that summer conducted the Cäcilien-Verein and had fallen in love with Cécile Jeanrenaud. He wanted to clear his mind, but he took with him a page of her sketches (now in this sketch-book, fol. 3) and seems (from letters to his friend Ferdinand Hillier) to have thought of her constantly. When he returned to Frankfurt they became engaged. The Dutch holiday was a period of acute boredom, and perhaps the meticulous detail of his drawings reflects the sense of the weight of time on his hands. Other occupations were a daily lesson from Schadow in drawing figures, and attempts to encourage Schadow's son to swim and to learn his Latin.

20. MS. M. Deneke Mendelssohn c. 21, fol. 19. L. von Beethoven: Ecossaise in D major, WoO 22.
Beethoven composed this Ecossaise while staying at Baden near Vienna in the summer of 1810. Its presence in the album given by Mendelssohn to Cécile for her Christmas present, 1836, is due to Aloys Fuchs, the great autograph collector, from whom Mendelssohn also acquired at the same time the pieces by Haydn and Mozart which are contained in the same album.

21. MS. M. Deneke Mendelssohn c. 21, fol. 51. 'Tipti. dari. grapti. klapti. fausti?', children's game, by Philipp Veit. Given to Cécile by F. M. B. in her Christmas album, 1836. Pencil, sepia, and grey wash on grey paper.
Philipp Veit was F. M. B.'s cousin, the son of Abraham Mendelssohn's sister

Dorothea by her first, unhappy, marriage. She afterwards married Friedrich von Schlegel, and after his death in 1829 Philipp Veit lived with his widowed mother in Frankfurt, where in 1831 he became director of the Städel Institute. There is a pencil sketch by him of Cécile Jeanrenaud as a girl. He died in 1877. Cf. note to plate 15.

22. MS. M. Deneke Mendelssohn e. 6, fol. 25. A page from the diary which Cécile wrote and F. M. B. illustrated on their honeymoon. Wednesday, 10 May 1837.
They are in the Church of the Holy Ghost at Heidelberg on 8 May, F. M. B. conducting while Cécile's cousin Fritz Schlemmer plays the organ. Cécile and the unnamed lady appear to be giving their whole attention to Felix. The entry for Wednesday records rain and wind: 'fortunately Fritz brings newspapers and books with which we can pass the time: At 12 the two men go back to the organ. . . .'

23. Diploma signed by Spohr. Owned by Miss H. C. Deneke.
F. M. B. was one of the original honorary members elected by the Deutscher National-Verein für Musik und ihre Wissenschaft in March 1839. The purpose of the society, described in its first *Jahrbuch*, was to achieve 'by teaching and by example a more general and thorough education in musical art, knowledge, and taste'. The society published Jahrbücher only from 1839 to 1841. Louis Spohr (1784–1859) was the first President.

24. Programme for a subscription concert in the Gewandhaus, Leipzig, 21 March 1839. Owned by Miss H. C. Deneke.
Mendelssohn became director of the Gewandhaus concerts in 1835 and continued in office to the end of his life. The first item in the programme of 21 March 1839 was the Great C major Symphony of Schubert, which was receiving its world premiere. The symphony was composed in 1828 and remained unperformed at the composer's death in the same year. On New Year's Day 1839 Schumann met Schubert's brother Ferdinand in Vienna, and was shown a number of unpublished manuscripts of his brother's music, including this symphony. News of the discovery was communicated to Mendelssohn, who decided to perform the Great C major Symphony during the current season of the Gewandhaus concerts.

25. Mus. 221 d. 422. Title-page of the Scotch Symphony, published 1843.
F. M. B. worked intermittently on his third symphony from the autumn of his journey to Scotland with Klingemann, 1829 (cf. 11, 12) until January 1841. It was first performed at the Gewandhaus, Leipzig, 3 March 1842, from manuscript score and parts. F. M. B. had these sent to England in April, and himself conducted a performance by the Philharmonic Society on 13 June. On this visit to England he twice saw Queen Victoria at Buckingham Palace, first on 20 June, and again on 9 July, in the last hour before the royal household left for Claremont. It was also the last day before the Mendelssohns were leaving for home. On this occasion the Queen was persuaded to sing one of the songs from F. M. B.'s *Zwölf Gesänge*, op. 8. The parrot was removed 'or he will scream louder than I can sing'—the Prince Consort rang

for a servant, 'and the Prince of Gotha said "I will carry him out", upon which I replied "Allow *me* to do that" (like cousin Wolf with his "Allow *me, me, me!*") and lifted up the big cage and carried it out to the astonished servants, etc. . . . And which did she choose?—"Schöner und schöner schmückt sich"—sang it quite charmingly in strict time and tune, and with very good execution. Only in the last line "Der Prosa Last und Müh", where it goes down to D and then comes up again so closely, she sang D sharp each time, and as I gave her the note the two first times, the last time she sang D, and there it ought to have been D sharp. But with the exception of this little mistake it was really charming, and the last G I have never heard better, or purer, or more natural from any amateur. Then I was obliged to confess that Fanny had written the song (which I found very hard, but pride must have a fall), and to beg her to sing one of my own also. . . . I must add that I begged the Queen to allow me to dedicate my A minor symphony to her. . . .' A later, more formal, request in writing seems to have survived only among papers endorsed by one of the family 'torn up drafts from the waste paper basket of F. M. B.'. When he wrote, the 4-hand arrangement for piano had been published, but he asked to be allowed to dedicate to her ('to lay at her feet') the full score.

26. MS. M. Deneke Mendelssohn c. 21, fol. 58, 'Montreux', 22 August 1843.
27. 'Chillon', 23 December 1843. Owned by Miss H. C. Deneke. Water-colours, from pencil sketches.

In the summer of 1842 F. M. B. and Cécile, with Paul Mendelssohn Bartholdy and his wife Albertine, went to Switzerland for a holiday, which included a music festival at Lausanne where the Hymn of Praise (op. 52) was performed. Two sketches done on 6 August, just after the festival, were copied in water-colour during the following year: 'Montreux' was for Cécile's album. Perhaps these water-colours helped Mendelssohn to acquire the technique which is unexpectedly evident in his last set of pictures of Switzerland, June–September 1847. The original sketch-book has at the beginning pictures of the four Mendelssohns and five friends they met at Interlaken, with the sitters' signatures. One of them was the actor Eduard Genast, whose impressions of F. M. B. are recorded in his published diary. He greatly enjoyed watching F. M. B. sketching (with extraordinary accuracy) Interlaken from a neighbouring height on 19 August. Genast describes F. M. B.'s extremely neat appearance: 'he looked, except for his [Italian straw] hat and strong shoes ['Alpenschuhe'] as if he could go straight to Court. We others looked very inelegant beside him.' On earlier travels there had been references to more informal dress and even to the growth of a beard.

28. Welcoming verse to F. M. B. on his arrival at the Zweibrücken Music Festival, 31 July 1844. Printed on silk. 495 × 360 mm. Owned by Miss H. C. Deneke.
For this festival F. M. B. interrupted for a week (31 July–6 August) a long family holiday in the peaceful countryside of Soden, near Frankfurt. He was perhaps the less encouraged to go because his younger sister Rebecka changed her mind about joining him there from Italy. He wrote to her in Sorrento, 'Vesuvius I must own has greater attraction. . . . Breiting [a friend from the time at Düsseldorf] will probably be one of

the singers but whether he is in as good a state of preservation as Pompeii, I am doubtful.' To his other sister he wrote, '. . . tomorrow week (God willing) I shall be back again. Then I shall once more lie down under the apple-trees, etc., *dal segno*. Ah! if it could always be like this.' The welcome of the inhabitants of Zweibrücken (a little town which after the troubles at the turn of the century can hardly have known whether to regard itself as Bavarian or French) and their painstakingly expressed thanks for his inspiration reflect the happiness engendered by such occasions.

29. MS. M. Deneke Mendelssohn d. 11, fol. 10. The family at Soden, 23 September 1844, by F. M. B.

The four children are Karl (6), Marie (nearly 5), Paul (3), and Felix, who died very young (then just over a year old). Lili was born the next year. An earlier version of the picture lacks the miniatures and the blackberry wreath. Some of the places in the decorative border were sketched in a book given to F. M. B. by Cécile's grandmother that summer: the church at Neuheim and the 'drei Linden' (always so called although only two survived) and (top right) the little town of Cronberg. Between the train and the steamer, Frankfurt is seen across the Main.

30. MS. M. Deneke Mendelssohn b. 2, fol. 52. F. Chopin: Ballade in F minor, op. 52.

The F minor Ballade, one of Chopin's finest works, was composed in 1842, but the autograph was considered lost until its recent discovery in Cécile's album, which Felix began for her Christmas present, 1844. Unfortunately only four pages are present, containing about half the work (bars 1–136). The album also contains an autograph fair copy of the same composer's Mazurka in A flat, op. 59 no. 2, specially written out for Cécile on 8 October 1845. Mendelssohn had first met Chopin in Berlin in 1828, and their friendship continued for the rest of Felix's life.

31. Letter from Robert Schumann to F. M. B. from Dresden, 9 February 1846. Owned by Miss H. C. Deneke.

In this letter Schumann tells F. M. B. of the birth of his second child Emil. On 12 February his op. 52, 'Ouverture Scherzo und Finale für Orchester', then still unpublished, was to be given its second performance at the Gewandhaus, after an interval of four years from the first performance. Schumann says, 'Ohne dies wäre ich vielleicht zum Donnerstag-Concert nach L. gekommen, nun natürlich nicht' ('But for this perhaps I should have come to Leipzig for Thursday's concert, now of course not'). Schumann had, with F. M. B., been made responsible for the teaching of composition and piano when the Leipzig Conservatorium was opened in April 1843. Gewandhaus performances of his music were numerous. In 1844 he retreated to Dresden, where he lived very quietly, and made his friends among the artists, and in particular with Mendelssohn's friend Eduard Bendemann (cf. 3c and 16, and note to 35), rather than the musicians. He had managed to recover 'the old lost longing for music' (as he wrote to the violinist David) and to acquire for a time some degree of tranquillity. To this period belongs the C major Symphony (op. 61), which was given its first performance by F. M. B. at the Gewandhaus, 5 November 1846.

32. MS. M. Deneke Mendelssohn c. 21, fol. 60ᵛ. Jenny Lind's contribution to Cécile's album, 11 April 1846.

'Saknad' is 'Loss' or 'Lack'. 'Jag hade en Wän', 'I had a friend', written on the eve of a concert she gave with F. M. B., Ferdinand David, and (as a last-minute innovation at F. M. B.'s unexpected request) Clara Schumann. This was at the Gewandhaus, 12 April 1846. Jenny Lind was to leave Leipzig for Vienna on the following day. It was after this that she first went to England, where her success was dazzling and she was called 'The Swedish Nightingale'. Her powers were perhaps first really apparent in Germany, where she sang her first opera part (Bellini's *Norma*) at Berlin in the winter of 1844. She and F. M. B. became intimate friends. He said of her to Hans Andersen, 'There will not be born, in a whole century, another being so gifted as she', and the principal soprano part of the *Elijah* (cf. 33) was written with her voice in mind. When after his death it was decided that the Mendelssohn Scholarship should be founded in memory of him, and that funds should be raised in England by a performance of *Elijah*, Jenny Lind at last took part. She assisted at all rehearsals, and after the performance (Exeter Hall, London, 15 December 1848) she wrote to Cécile: 'How the good English have understood and absorbed this particular music! As for myself, I sing it in quite a special mood.' Many years later she helped her husband Otto Goldschmidt in training the London Bach Choir for the first performance in England of the B minor Mass of J. S. Bach, 26 April 1876. She died in 1887.

33. Vocal score of the *Elijah* in the hands of F. M. B. and his translator, William Bartholomew. Dated at the end 26 February 1847. Owned by Miss H. C. Deneke.

In this manuscript F. M. B. wrote his arrangement for piano of the orchestral parts, and so much of the English words as had been decided upon, in ink. He wrote in pencil German words where translation was still needed. Bartholomew wrote English words (they are in red ink) and, if he had to, altered the note values.

The history of the *Elijah* covers nearly ten years. F. M. B. had decided after the success of his *St. Paul* at Düsseldorf in 1836 to write another oratorio, and already on 18 February 1837 was writing to Klingemann (who was to provide words) with suggestions of the treatment—dramatic? epic? or both?—he wanted. While he was in London in September 1837 he spent two mornings with Klingemann at work on a draft (he drew the room in which they had worked, with a piano and a big round table, in Cécile's honeymoon diary). Klingemann's draft was in the end sent to F. M. B. unfinished, and he turned to Pastor Julius Schubring, who selected instead passages from the Old Testament. It was not until February 1845 that F. M. B. actively engaged himself on the music with a definite end in view—a first performance, to be conducted by himself, at the Birmingham Festival, August 1846. He worked at high pressure, and an extra difficulty was the translation. Bartholomew's almost impossible task was to find phrases, as close as possible to those of the English autho-rized version, to lie without distortion where the German words had first been intended. They were only just ready in time, and the parts for the final chorus were received nine days before the performance. Soloists and orchestra, and of course F. M. B. himself, read from manuscript. Though the principal soprano part was composed for Jenny Lind, she did not come to England on this occasion, and sang the part only after F. M. B.'s death (cf. 32). The score was much altered after the first performance and changes were still being made at the time when F. M. B. and Bartholomew were preparing the vocal score for publication.

34. 'Altdeutsches Frühlingslied', op. posth. 86 no. 6. In F. M. B.'s hand, dated 7 October 1847. Owned by Miss H. C. Deneke.

This is the end of F. M. B.'s last composition, finished less than a month before his death. The words are by the early seventeenth-century Jesuit poet Friedrich von Spee. They bear much the same meaning as Shelley's lament for Keats in *Adonais*:

> Winter is come and gone,
> But grief returns with the revolving year;
> The airs and streams renew their joyous tone;
> The ant, the bees, the swallows re-appear . . .

Conjecture has identified F. M. B.'s choice of the words with the death of his sister Fanny on 14 May that year.

35. MS. M. Deneke Mendelssohn b. 2, fol. 115$^\mathrm{v}$. Anonymous studies of F. M. B. on his deathbed. Pencil on brown paper.

F. M. B. died at Leipzig on 4 November 1847. Cécile sent for their friends at Dresden, Eduard Bendemann, Julius Hubner, Eduard Devrient, and the sculptor Ernst Rietschel. She wanted Rietschel to make a bust of her husband, and Bendemann to draw him. Finished pictures by both Bendemann and Hübner exist, as well as one by Wilhelm Hensel. Bendemann wrote to their mutual friend J. G. Droysen, 'The expression of his face was indescribably friendly and peaceful.' Rietschel's bust is at the Mendelssohn Archiv in Berlin.

36, 37. Cast of F. M. B.'s hand, his baton, and death mask.

Casts were taken for the children of F. M. B. The baton is ivory and ebony, tipped with silver. On his first visit to London in 1829, F. M. B. had a 'white stick' made, to conduct his Symphony in C minor (op. 11) for the Philharmonic Society: 'The maker took me for an alderman and would insist on decorating it with a crown.' Though Spohr and Weber had both used a baton in England before F. M. B., they were not in general use here before 1832–3, and F. M. B. thought some of the orchestra 'perhaps laughed a little, that this small fellow with the stick should take the place of their regular powdered and bewigged conductor' (referring to J. B. Cramer).

In February 1843, after Berlioz had conducted a concert of his own music at the Gewandhaus, F. M. B. gave him what Fanny Hensel described as his own 'pretty white stick of whalebone covered with white leather'. Berlioz is said to have returned 'an enormous cudgel of lime-tree with the bark on' with a letter which began, 'Great

chief! We have promised to exchange tomahawks! Here is mine, it is coarse, yours is
simple. ('Le mien est grossier, le tien est simple.') Only squaws and pale-faces like
ornate weapons. Be my brother, and when the Great Spirit has sent us to hunt in the
Land of Souls, may our warriors hang up our tomahawks together on the door of the
Council Chamber.'

slightly enlarged 9:8

1. Portrait of F. M. B. by Carl Begas, 1821

approx. 1:2

2. Harmony exercise with Zelter, 1819

3(*a*) Caricature of F. M. B. and Paul

slightly reduced

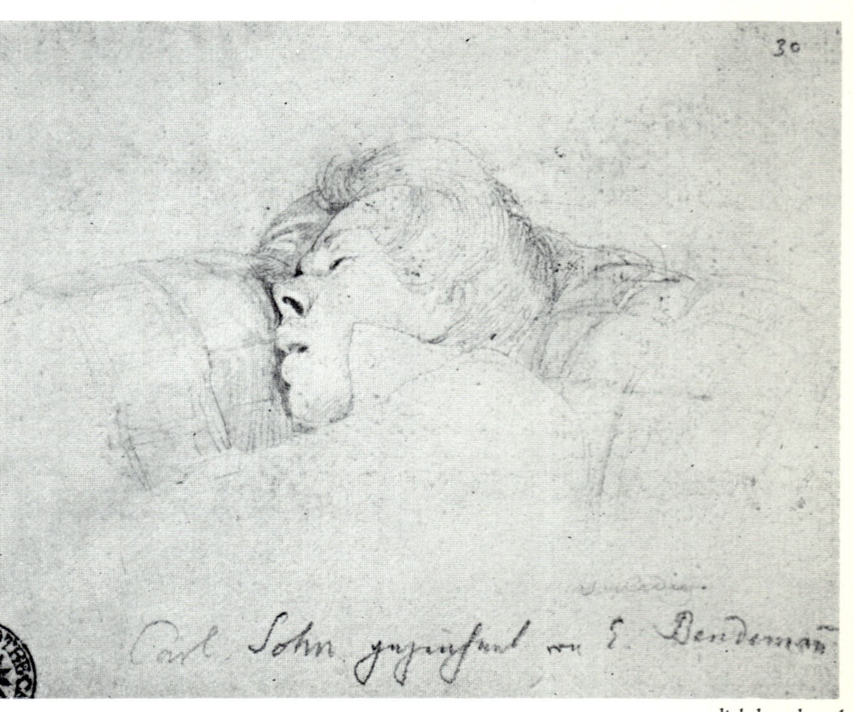

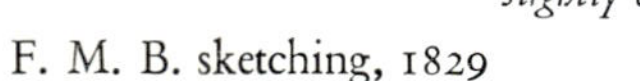

slightly enlarged

3(*b*) F. M. B. sketching, 1829

slightly enlarged

3(*c*) Carl Sohn by E. Bendemann, *c.* 1830–2

4. 'Jacob's Ladder', 1821

slightly reduced

5. Goethe's drawing of Eurydice

approx. 3:5

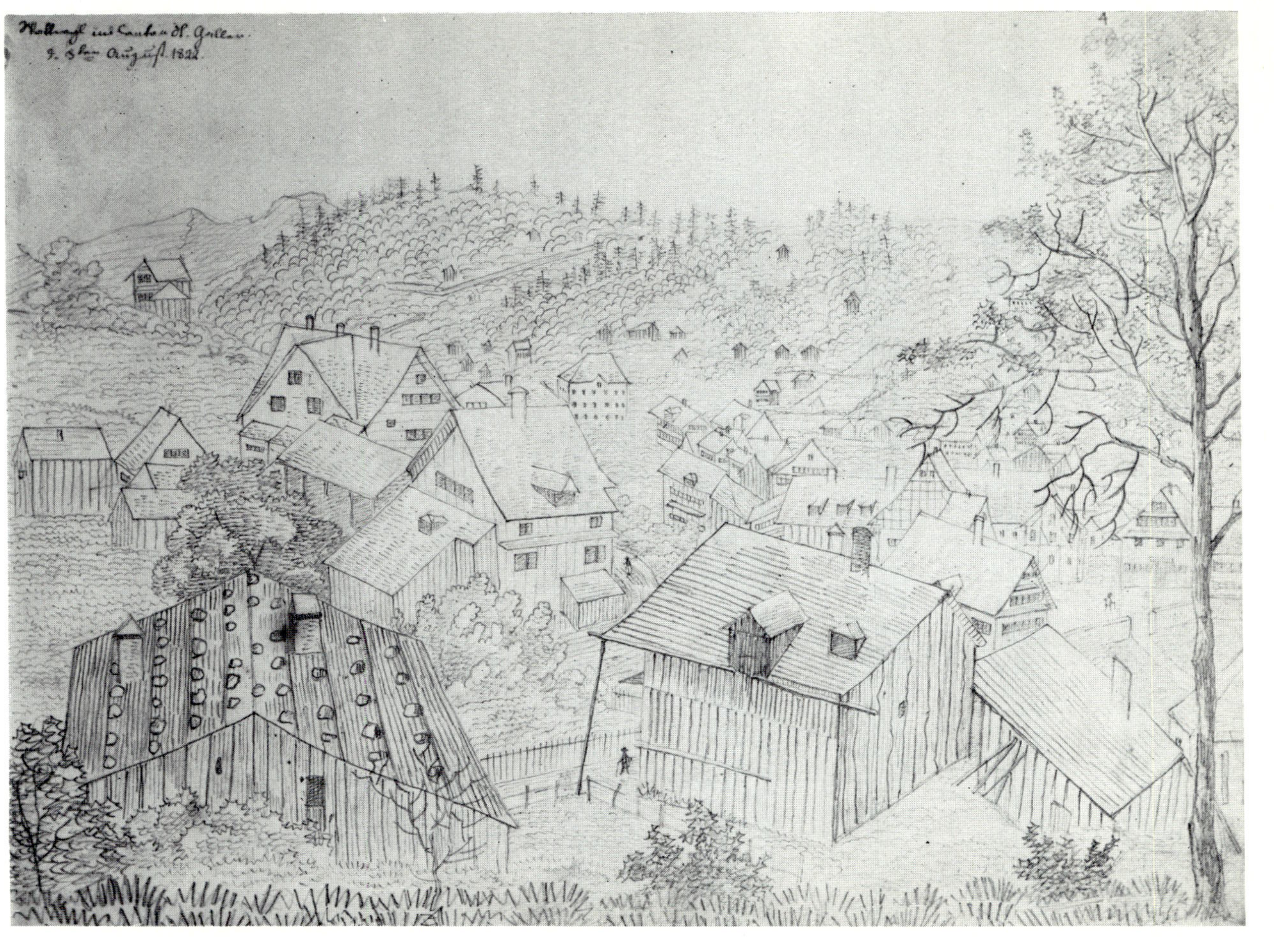

6. Wattwyl, 1822

approx. 1:2

7. Midsummer Night's Dream, Overture, 1826

approx. 2:3

8. Coburg, 1827

approx. 5:7

9. Coblenz, 1827

approx. 2:3

10. Score of St. Matthew Passion

approx. 1:2

approx. 5:8

11. Durham Cathedral, 1829

12. View towards the Hebrides, 1829

approx. 3:5

approx. 4:7

13. Telford's bridge, Conway, August 1829

14. Bavaria, July 1830

approx. 2:3

approx. 3:5

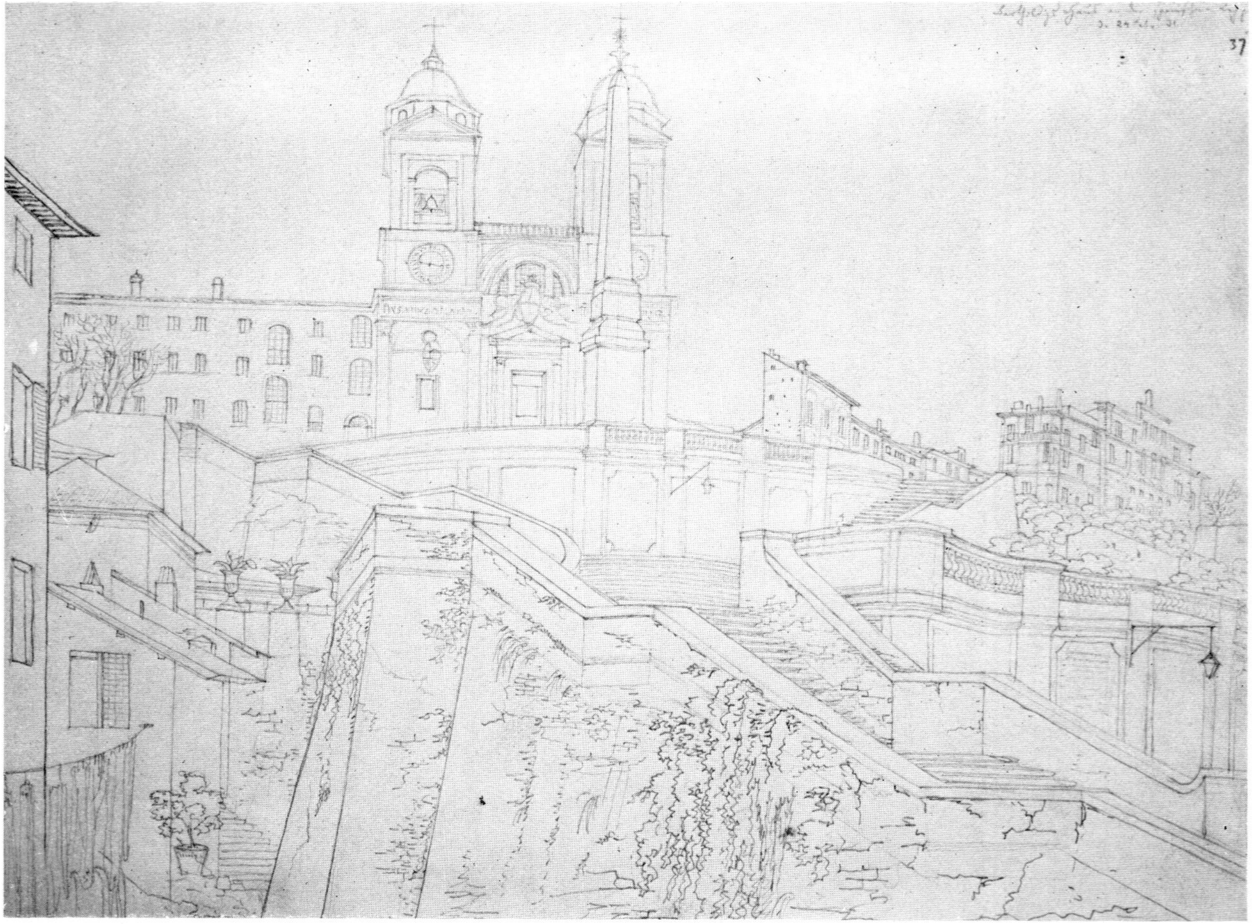

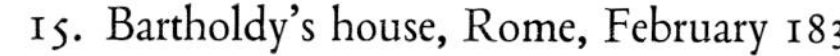

15. Bartholdy's house, Rome, February 1831

approx. 5:7

16. E. Bendemann, 'Bei Don Tommaso', May 1831

17. Amalfi, May 1831

approx. 2:3

approx. 5:9

18. 'Der klyne Groenmarkt, Haag', August 1836

19. 'Dampfboot der Zeeuw', August 1836

approx. 5:9

approx. 5:8

20. Beethoven, Ecossaise in D major. Autograph

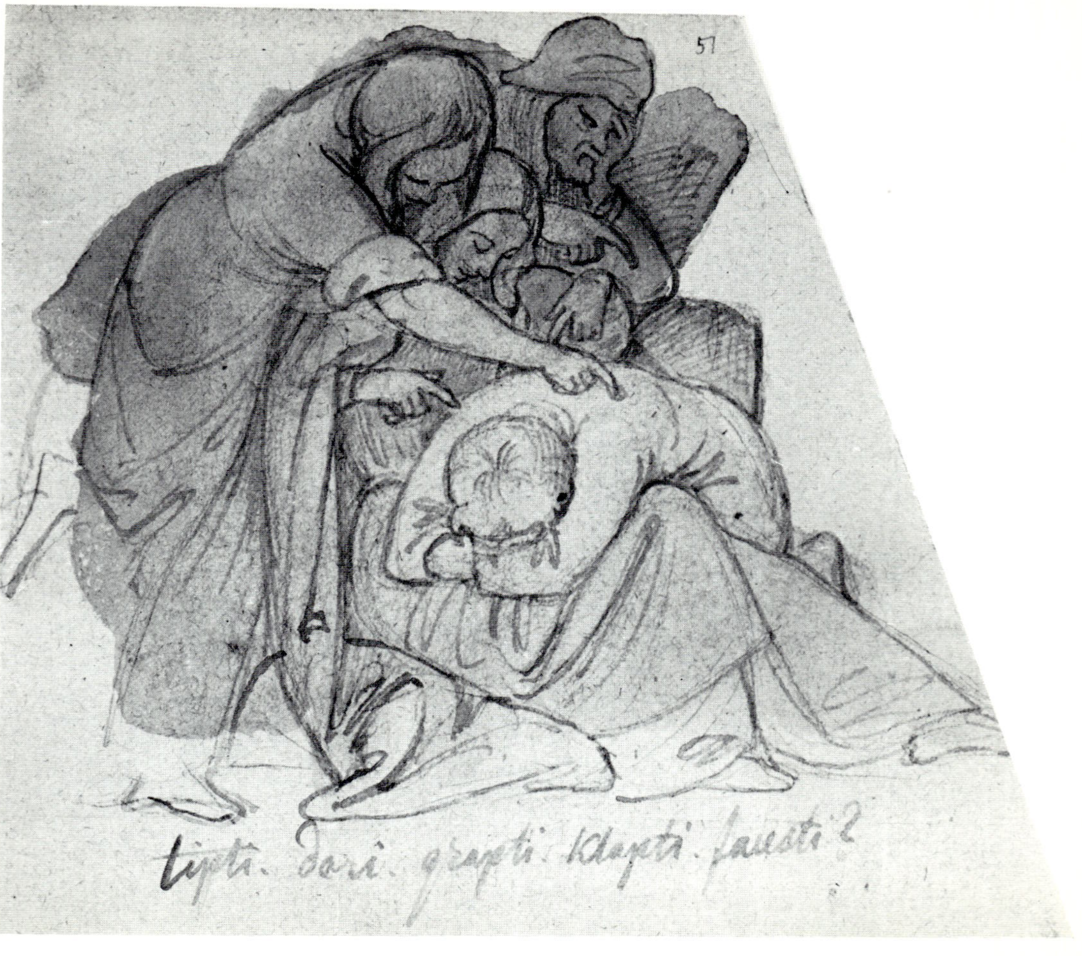

21. P. Veit, sketch of children's game

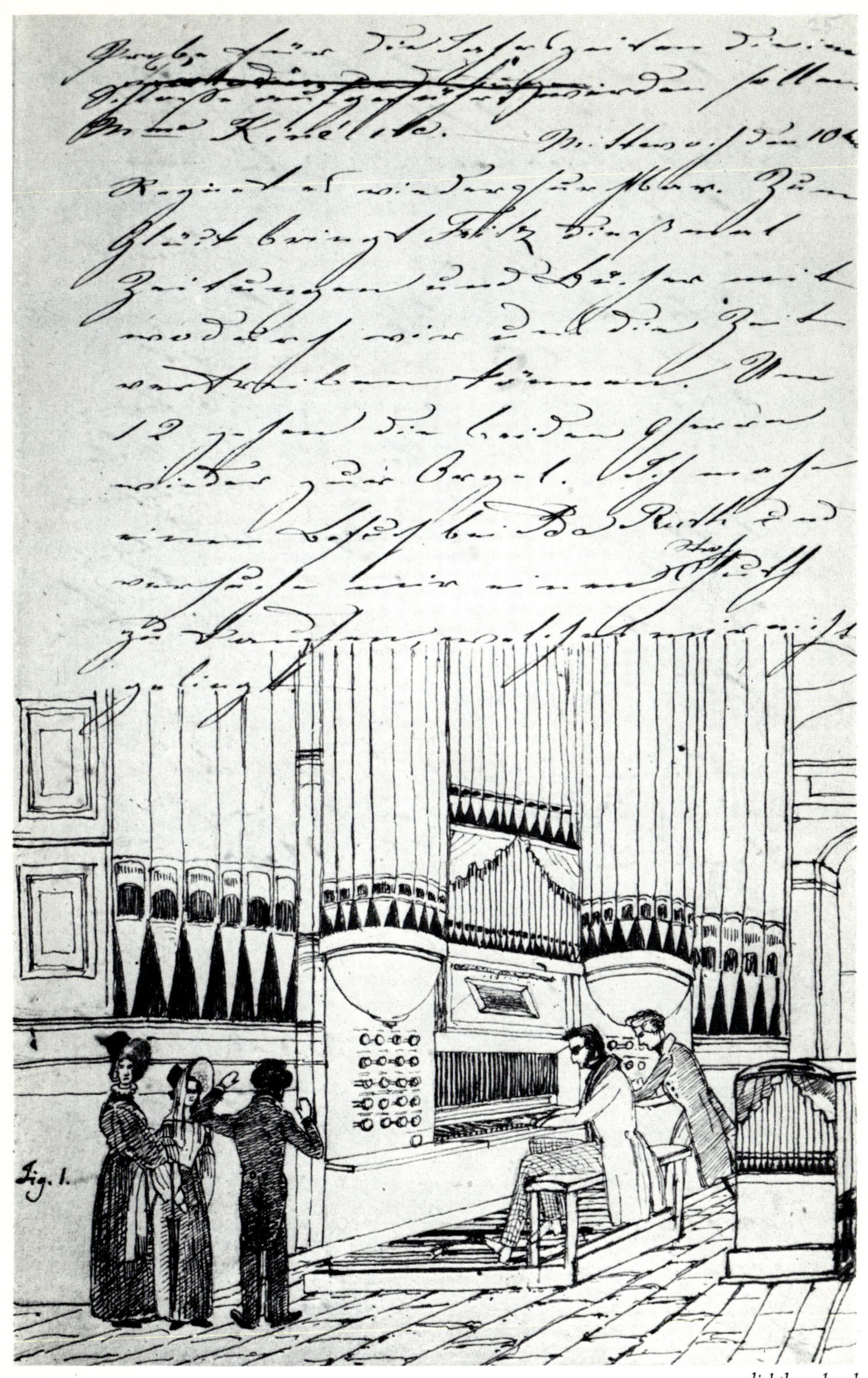

22. Heidelberg, honeymoon diary, 1837

slightly reduced

Omnia — ad majorem — Dei — gloriam.

DEUTSCHER NATIONAL-VEREIN
FÜR
MUSIK UND IHRE WISSENSCHAFT.

Der deutsche National-Verein für Musik und ihre Wissenschaft beschloss, nach §§. 3 — 12 der Statuten, ... F. Mendelsohn-Bartholdy zu Leipzig, zu seinem ... Mitgliede zu ernennen, und beauftragte unterzeichneten Präsidenten und permanenten Secretair, darüber gegenwärtiges Diplom auszustellen und zu befördern.

Permanenter Secretair des Vereins

Dr. Gustav Schilling

Derzeit. Präsident des deutschen National-Vereins f. M. u. ihre W.

Dr. Louis Spohr

Druck der Ch. Th. Groos'schen Buchdruckerei.

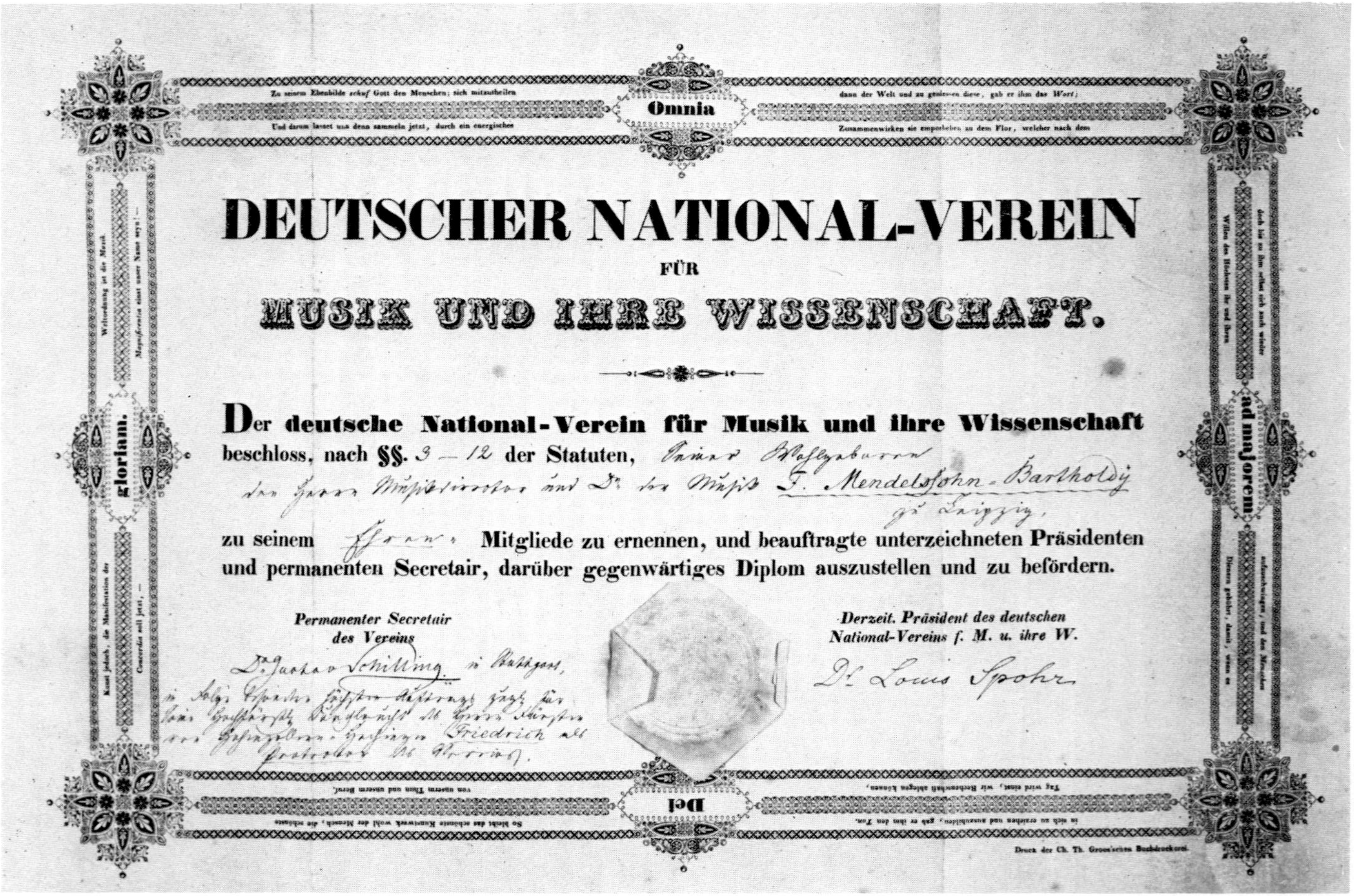

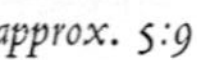

approx. 5:9

23. Diploma of the Deutscher National-Verein für Musik, 1839

Zwanzigstes
ABONNEMENT-CONCERT

im Saale des Gewandhauses zu Leipzig,

Donnerstag, den 21. März 1839.

(Die Ausführung der Chöre hat eine Anzahl hiesiger Dilettanten gütigst übernommen.)

***

Erster Theil.

***Grosse Symphonie* von Franz Schubert (C dur. Manuscript).**

***Der 42ste Psalm*, componirt von Felix Mendelssohn-Bartholdy.**

(Das Sopran-Solo vorgetragen von Mad. Bünau.)

Chor.

Wie der Hirsch schreit nach frischem Wasser, so schreit meine Seele, Gott, zu Dir.

Sopran-Solo.

Meine Seele dürstet nach Gott, nach dem lebendigen Gotte. Wann werde ich dahin kommen, dass ich Gottes Angesicht schaue?
Meine Thränen sind meine Speise Tag und Nacht, weil man täglich zu mir saget: wo ist nun dein Gott?

Frauenstimmen.

Denn ich möchte gern hingehen mit dem Haufen und mit ihnen wallen zum Hause Gottes, mit Frohlocken und mit Danken unter den Haufen, die da feiern.

Männerstimmen.

Was betrübst du dich, meine Seele, und bist so unruhig in mir? Harre auf Gott, denn ich werde ihm noch danken, dass er mir hilft mit seinem Angesicht.

Sopran-Solo.

Mein Gott, betrübt ist meine Seele in mir, darum gedenke ich an Dich! Deine Fluthen rauschen daher, dass hier eine Tiefe und dort eine Tiefe brausen; alle deine Wasserwogen und Wellen gehn über mich.

Quintett.

Männerstimmen.	Der Herr hat des Tages verheissen seine Güte, und des Nachts singe ich zu ihm, und bete zu dem Gotte meines Lebens.
Sopran-Solo.	Mein Gott, betrübt ist meine Seele in mir; warum hast Du meiner vergessen? Warum muss ich so traurig gehn, wenn mein Feind mich drängt?

approx. 5:6

24. Gewandhaus concert programme, 1839

slightly reduced

25. Scotch Symphony, title-page, 1843

26. Montreux, 1843

approx. 2:3

27. Chillon, 1843

approx. 3:5

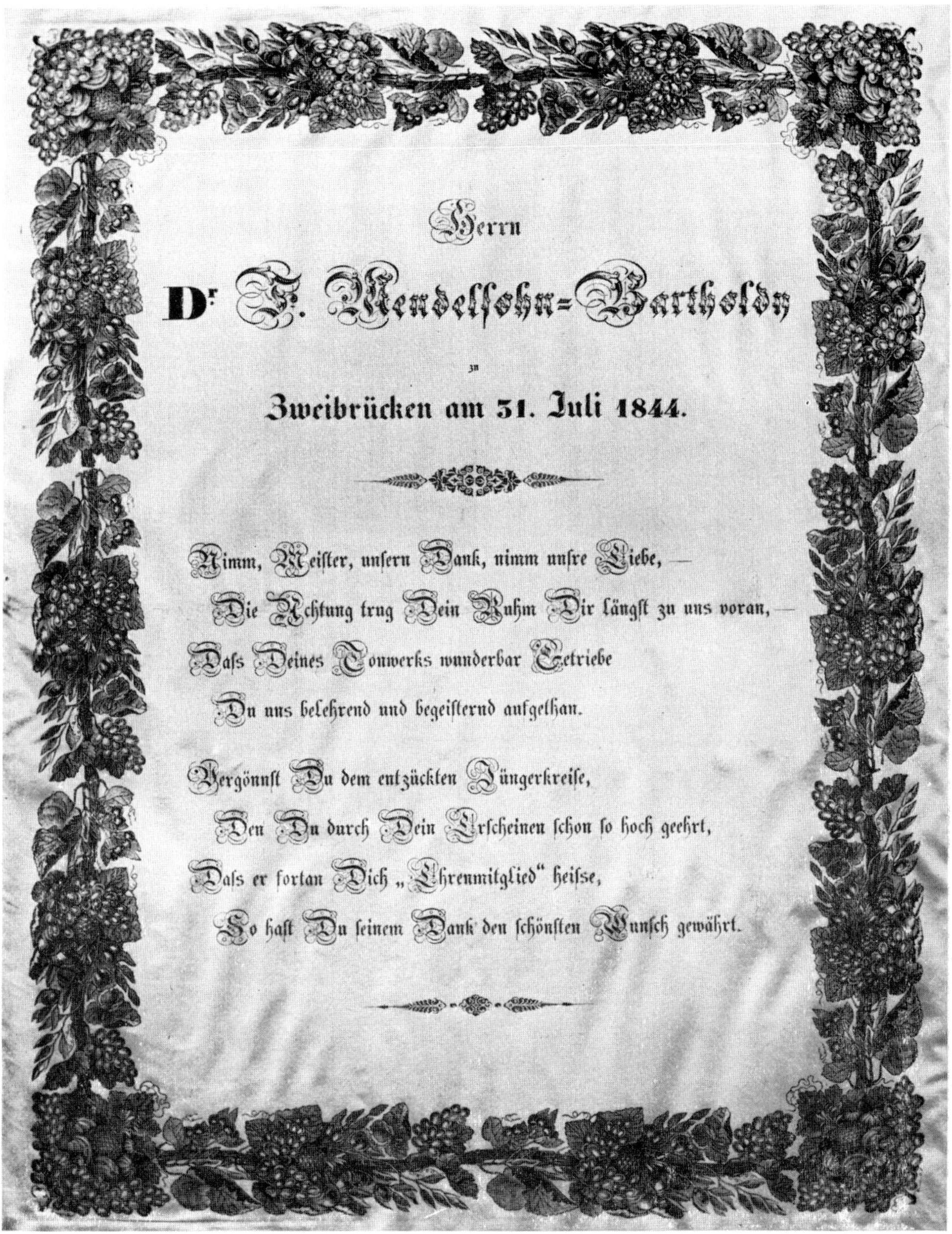

approx. 5:7

28. Zweibrücken festival, 1844

29. Soden, family picture, 1844

slightly reduced

30. Chopin, Ballade in F minor. Autograph

approx. 3:5

31. Schumann, Letter to F. M. B., 1846

32. Jenny Lind, autograph, 1846

33. *Elijah*, piano score with English words, 1847

approx. 3:4

34. F. M. B.'s last composition, 7 October 1847

approx. 2:3

35. Deathbed studies

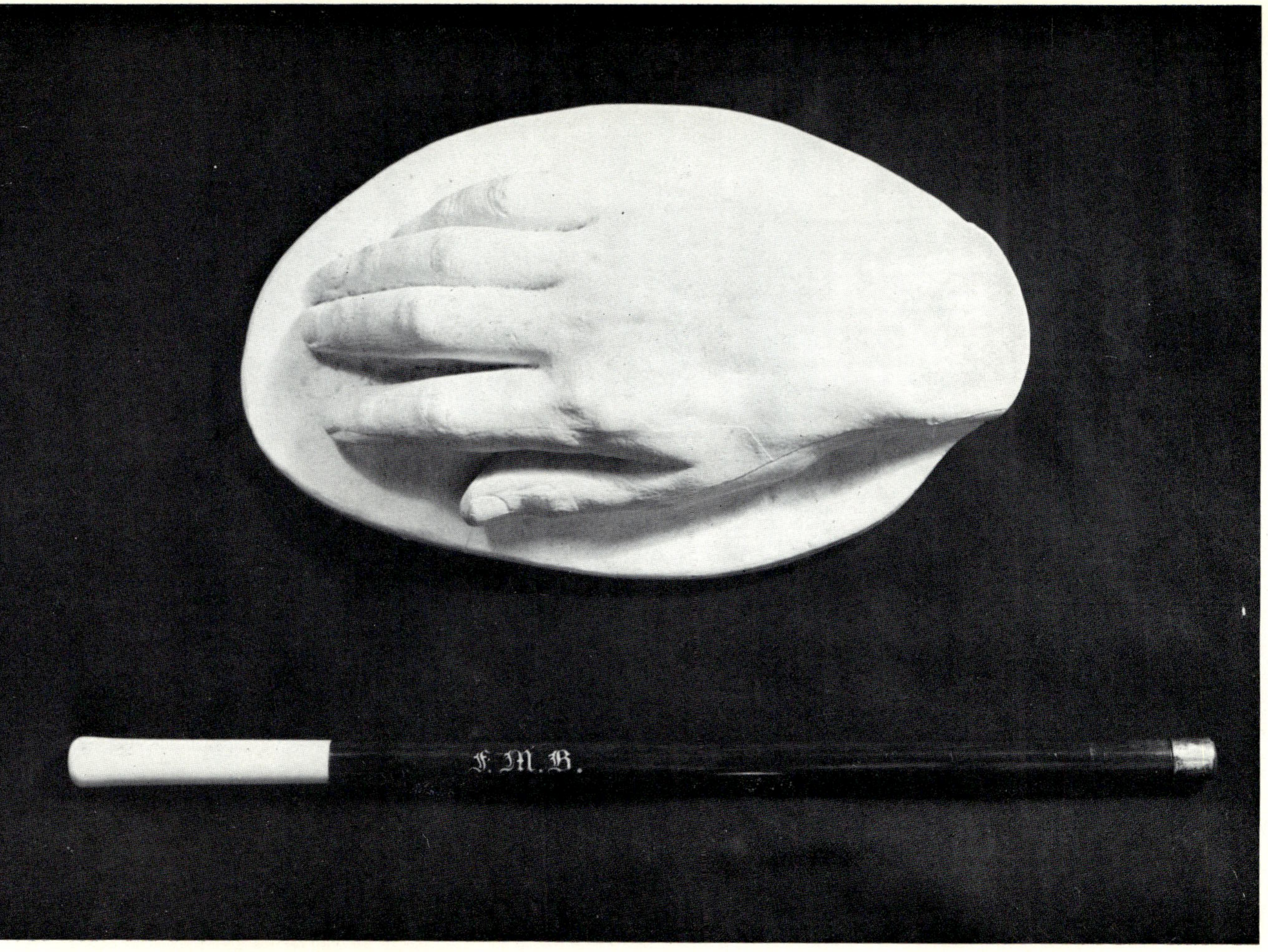

36. Cast of F. M. B.'s hand; presentation baton

37. Death mask